Puzzle Easter

Coloring Book

By

S.B. Nozaz

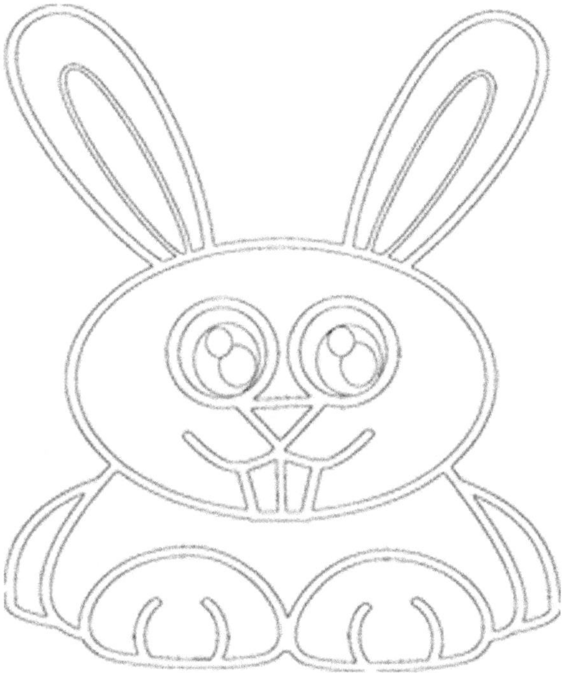

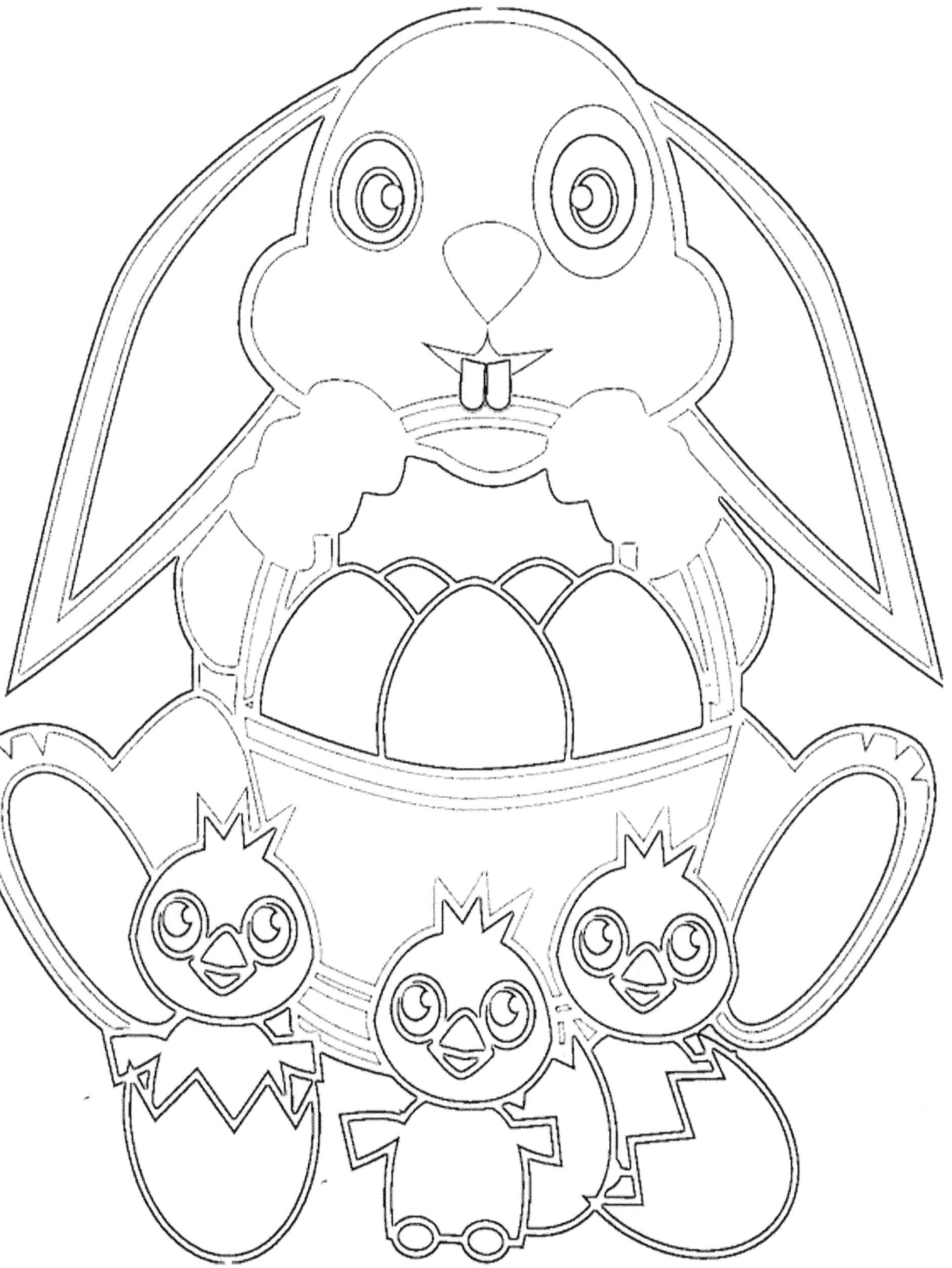

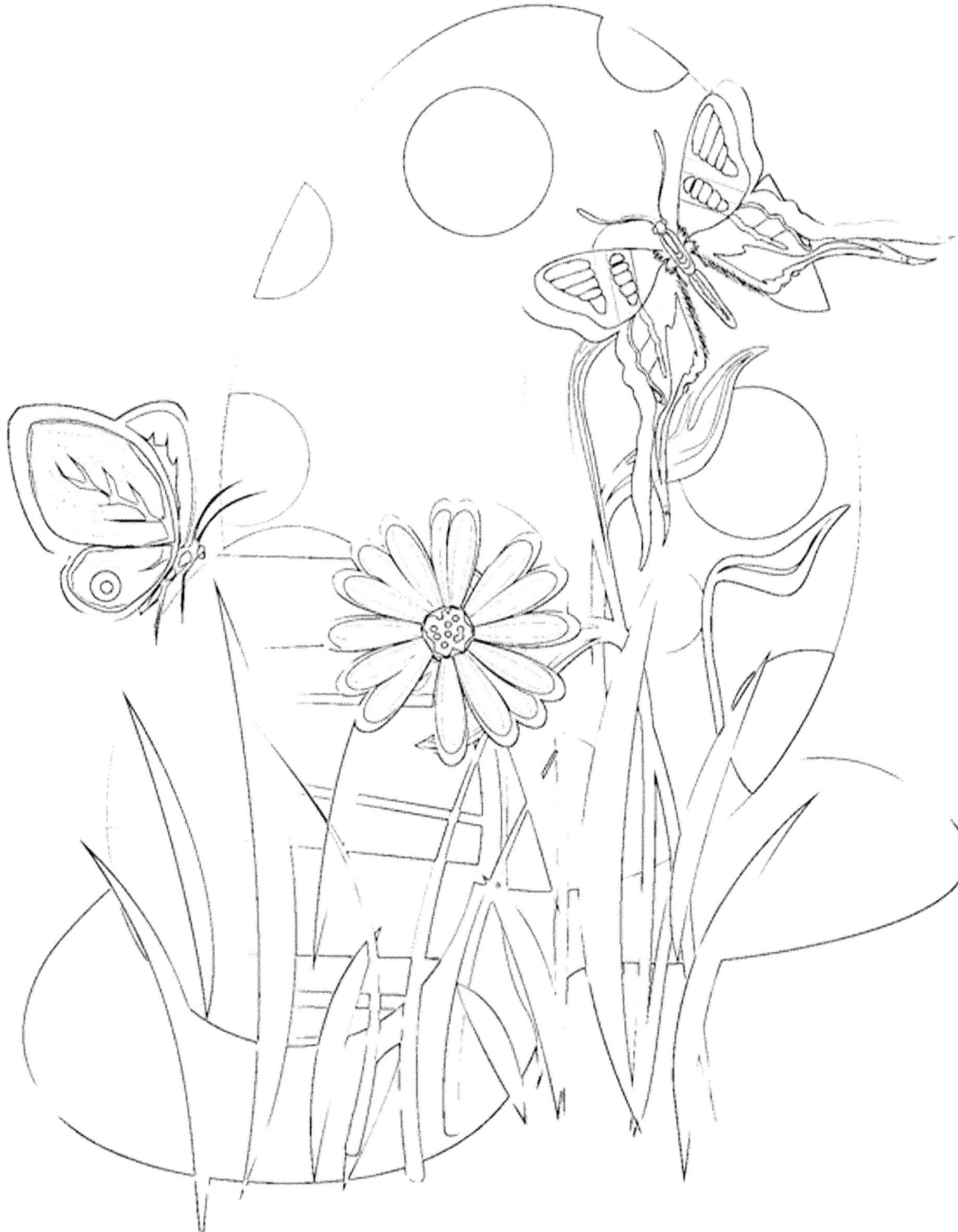

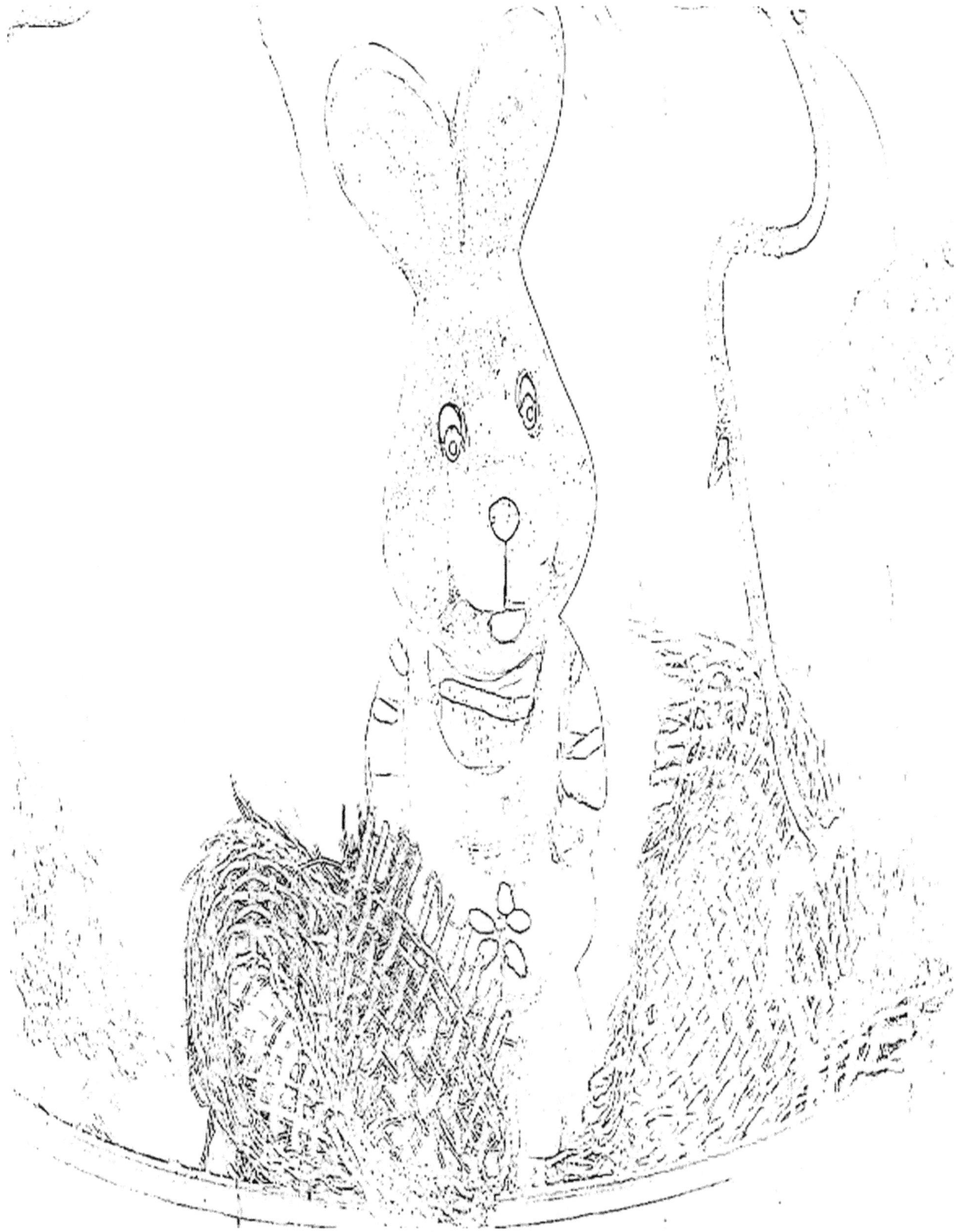

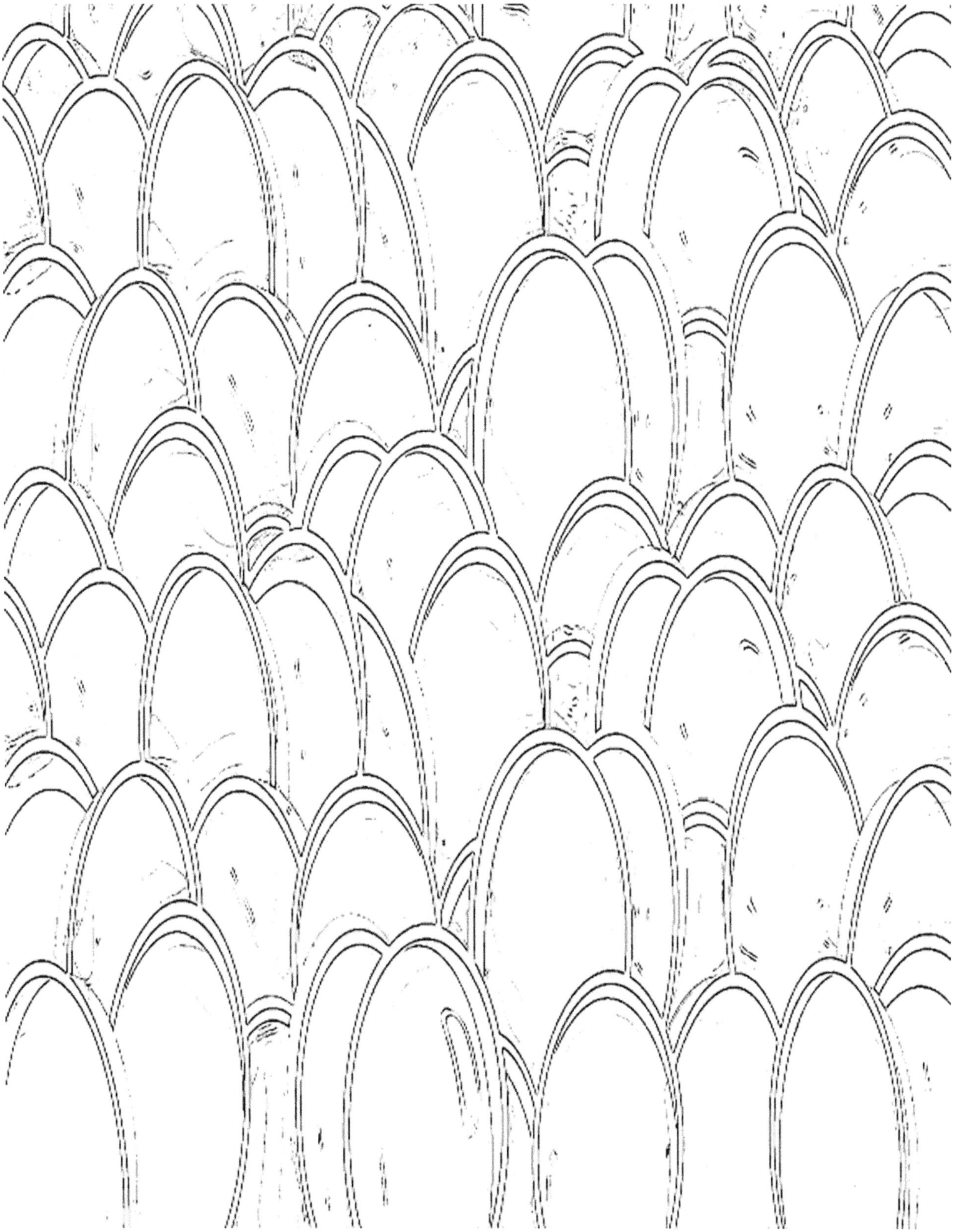

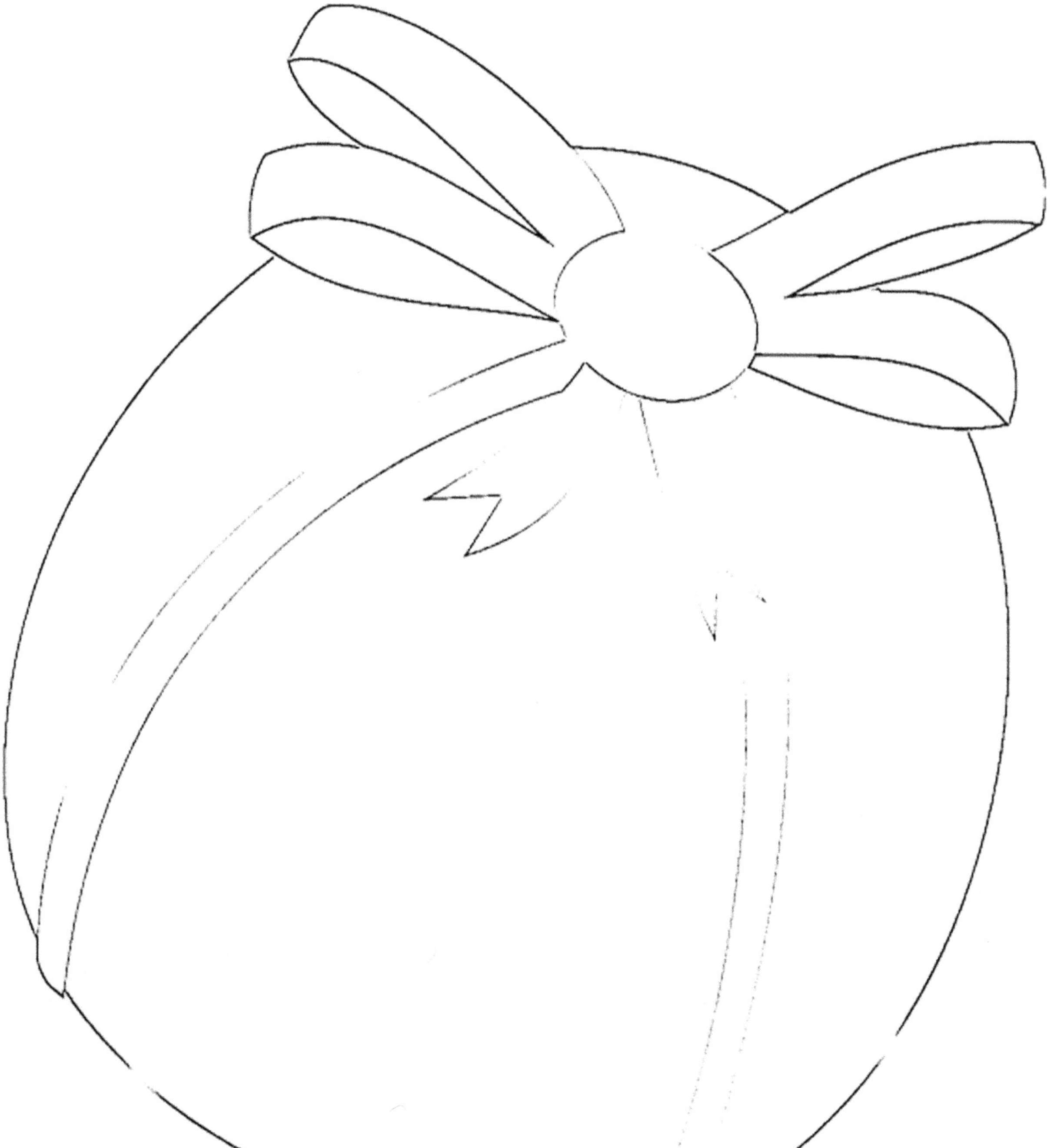

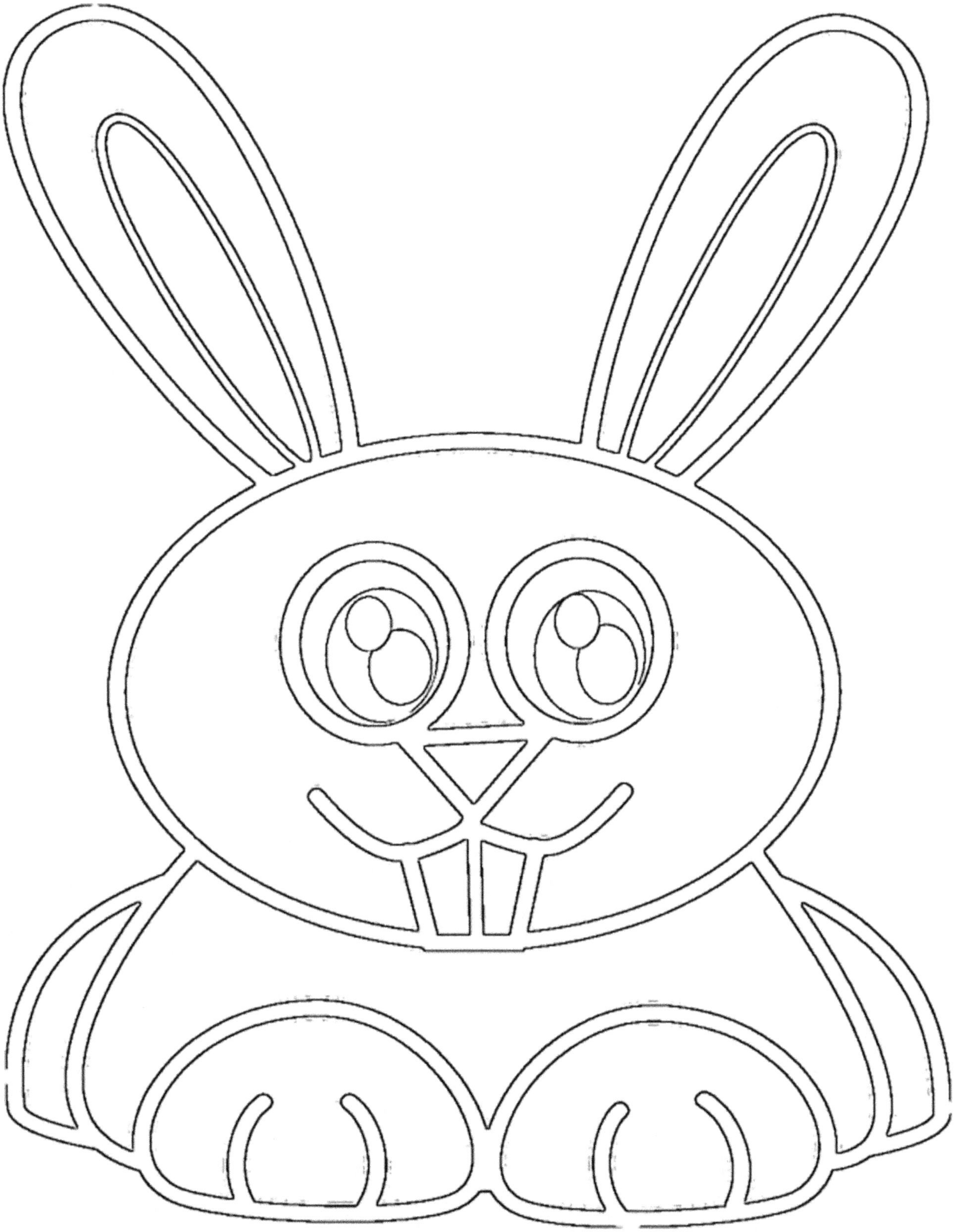

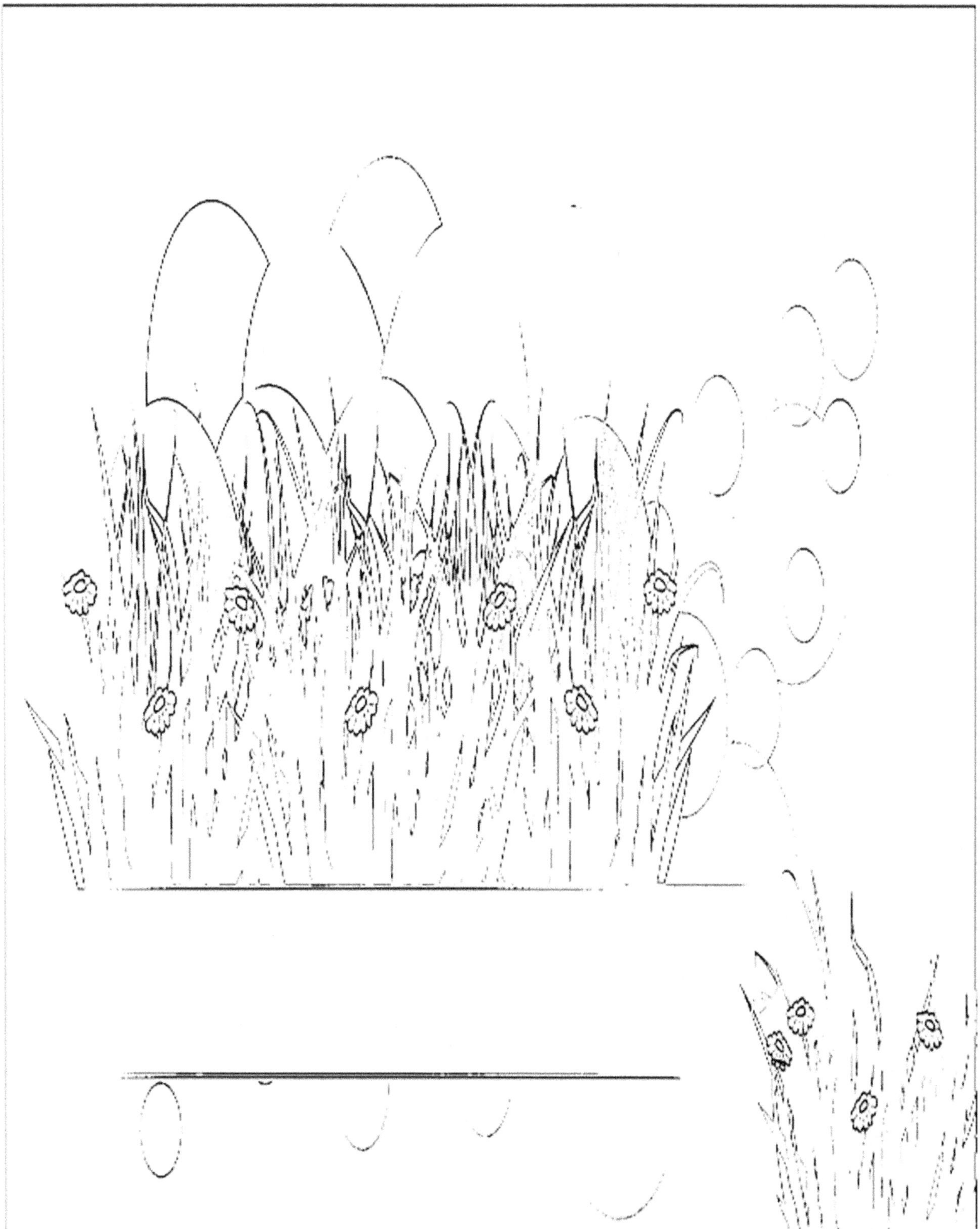

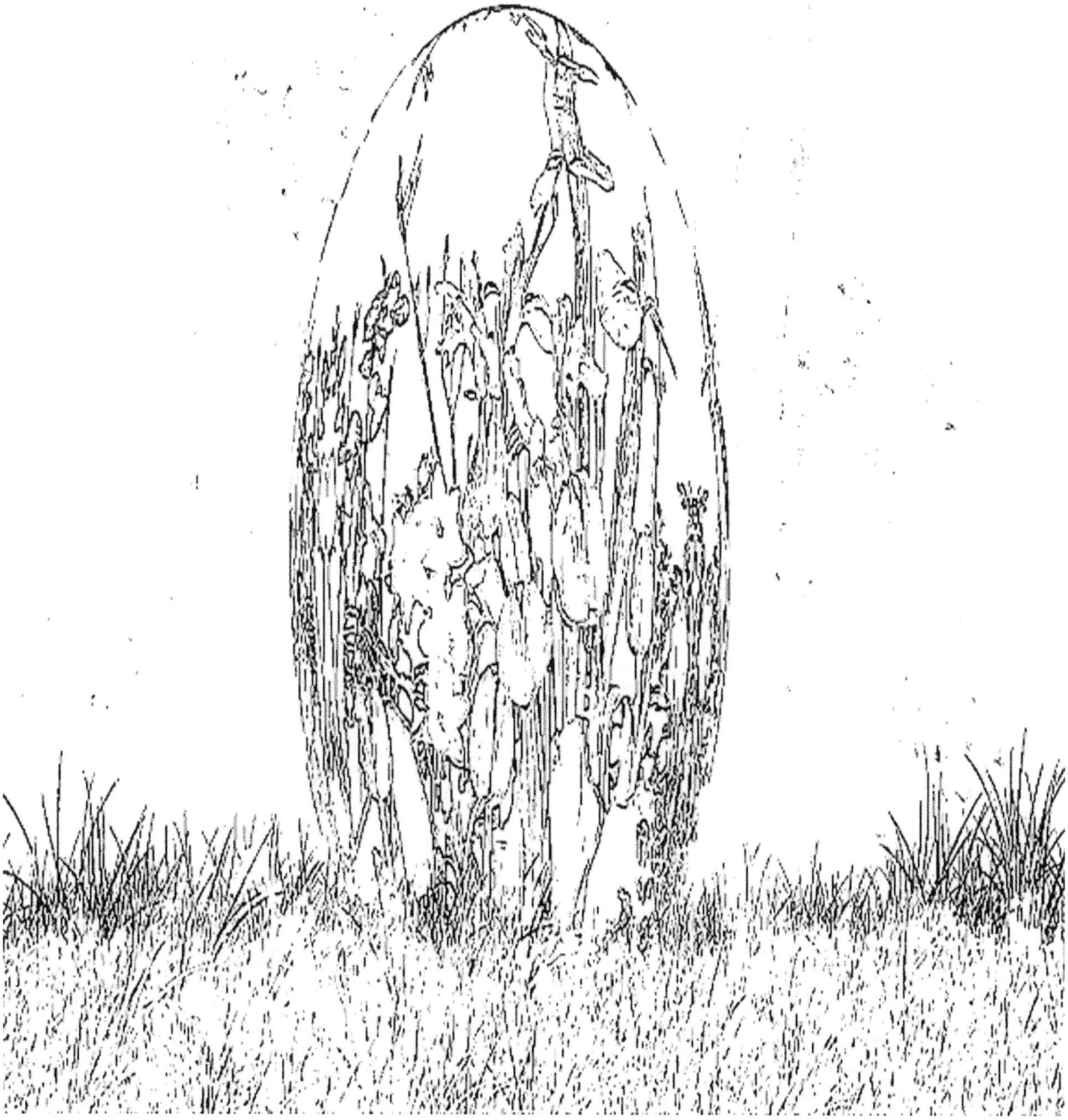

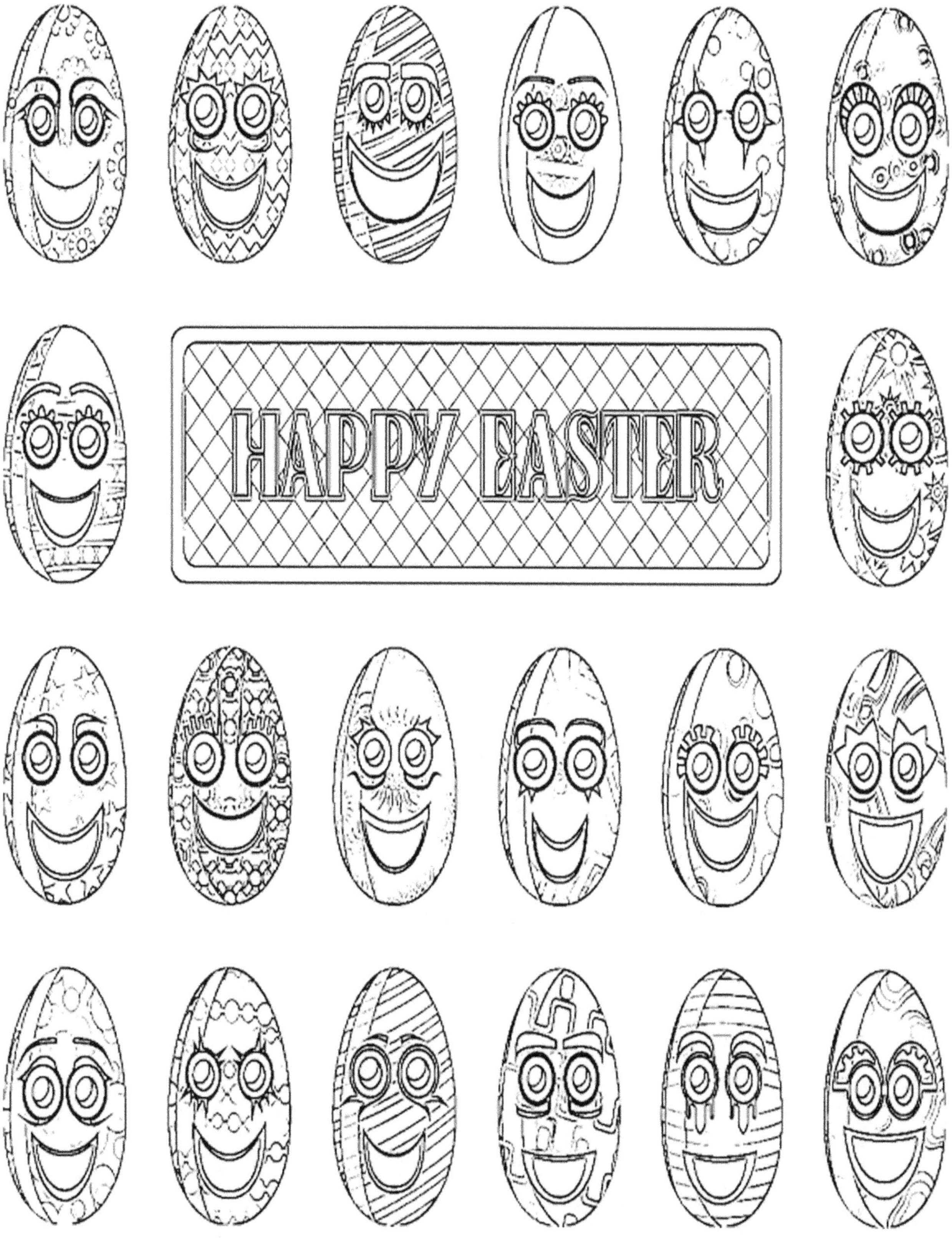
HAPPY EASTER

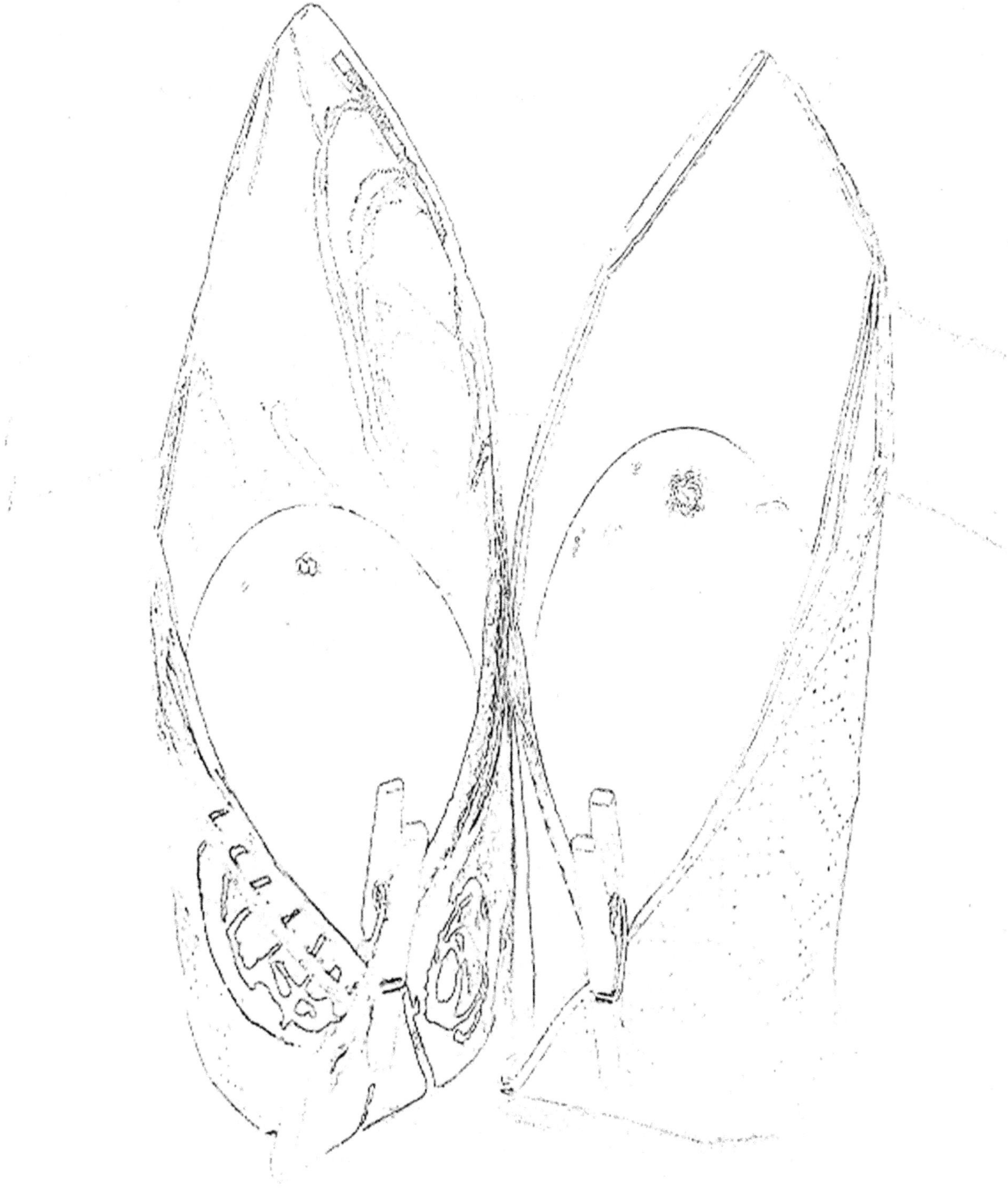

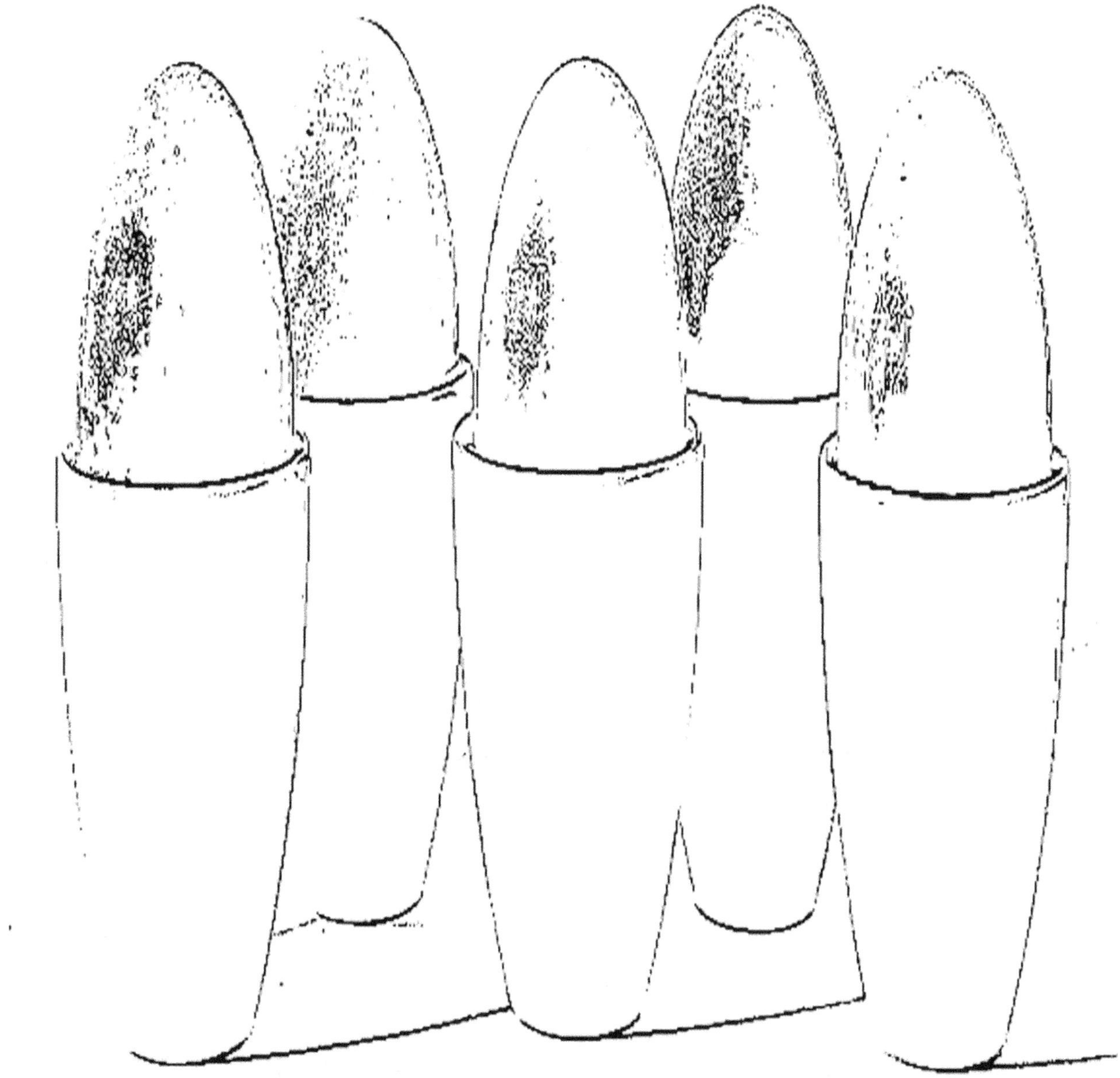

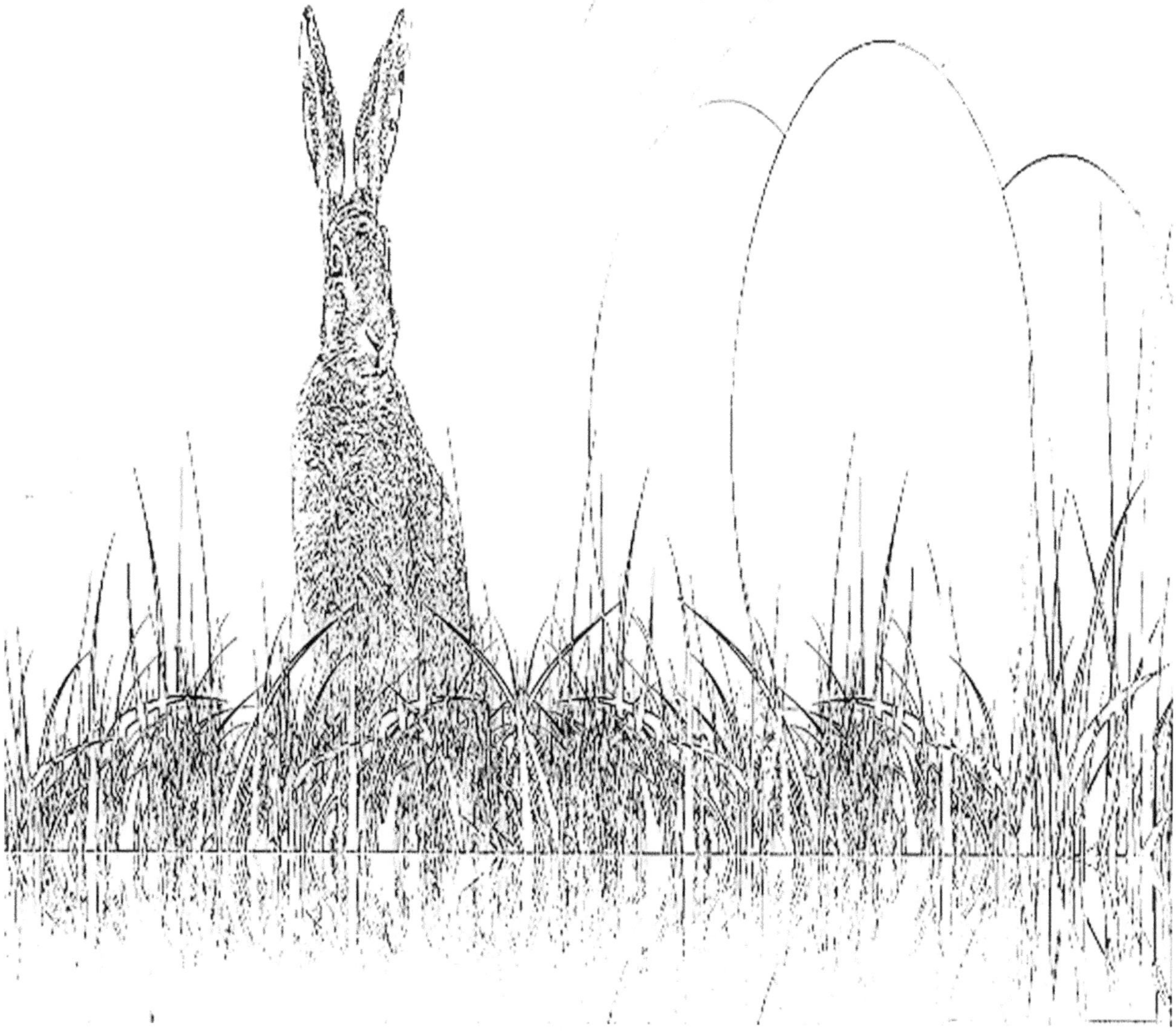

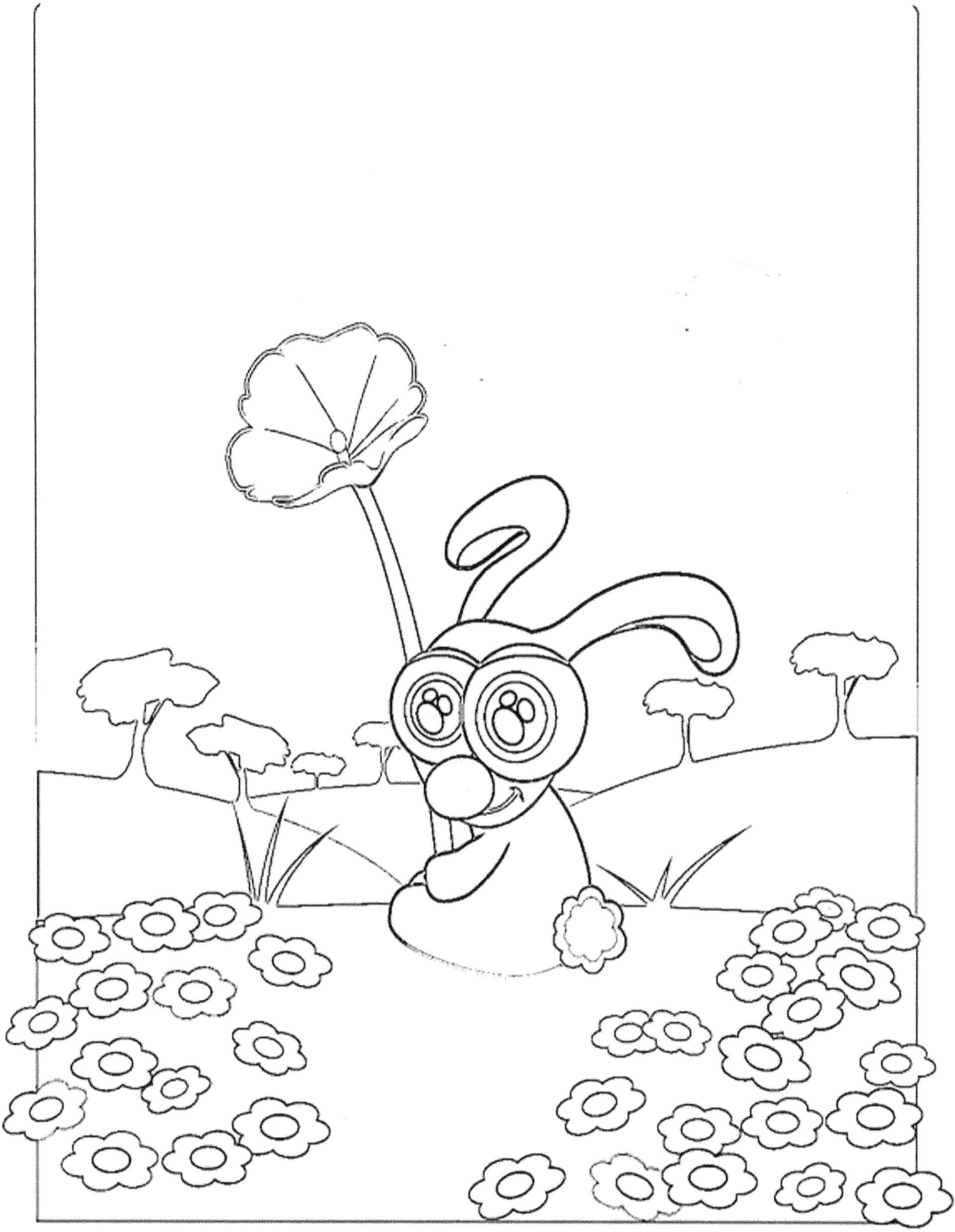

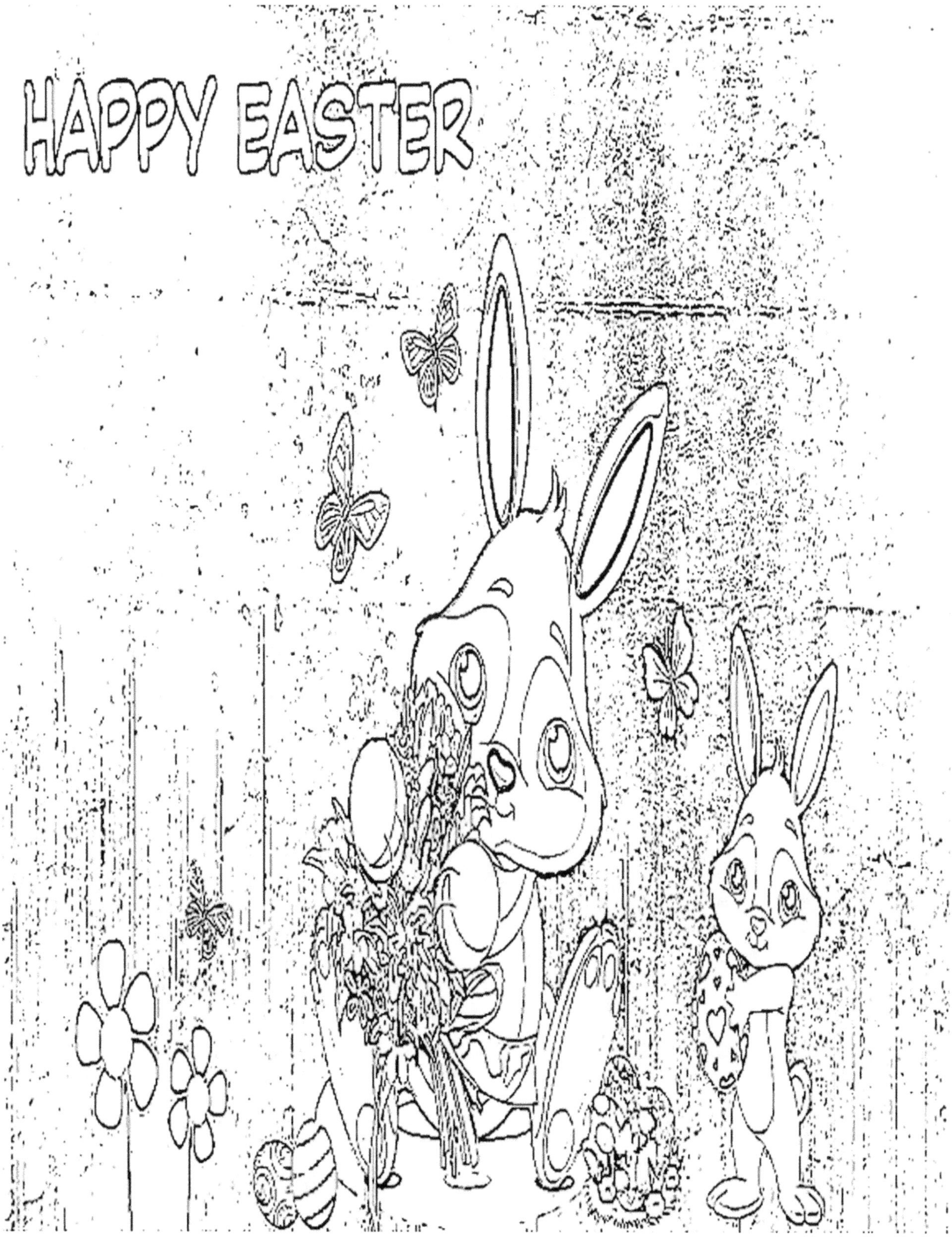
HAPPY EASTER

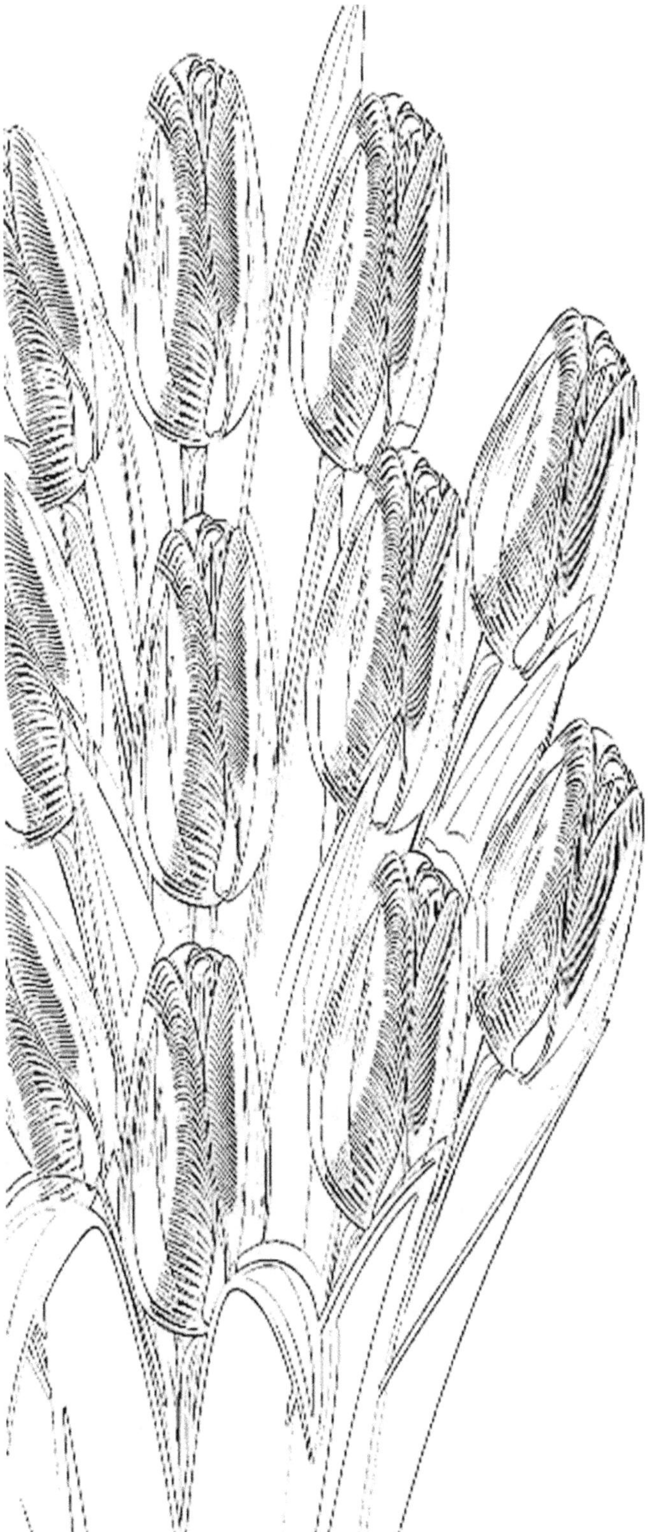
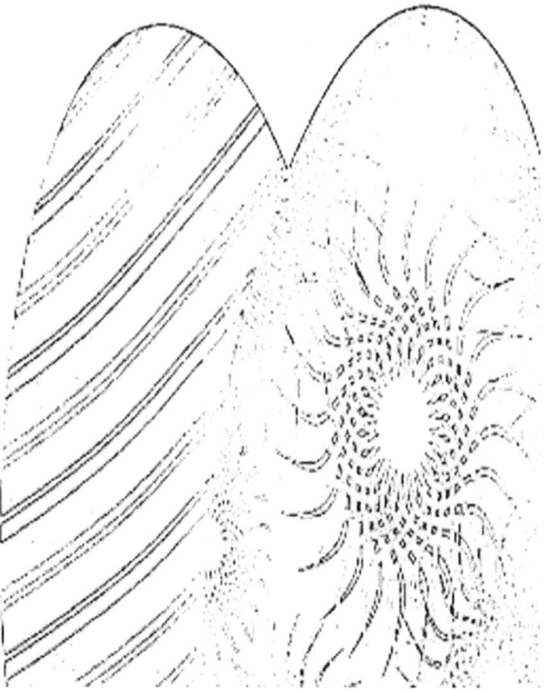

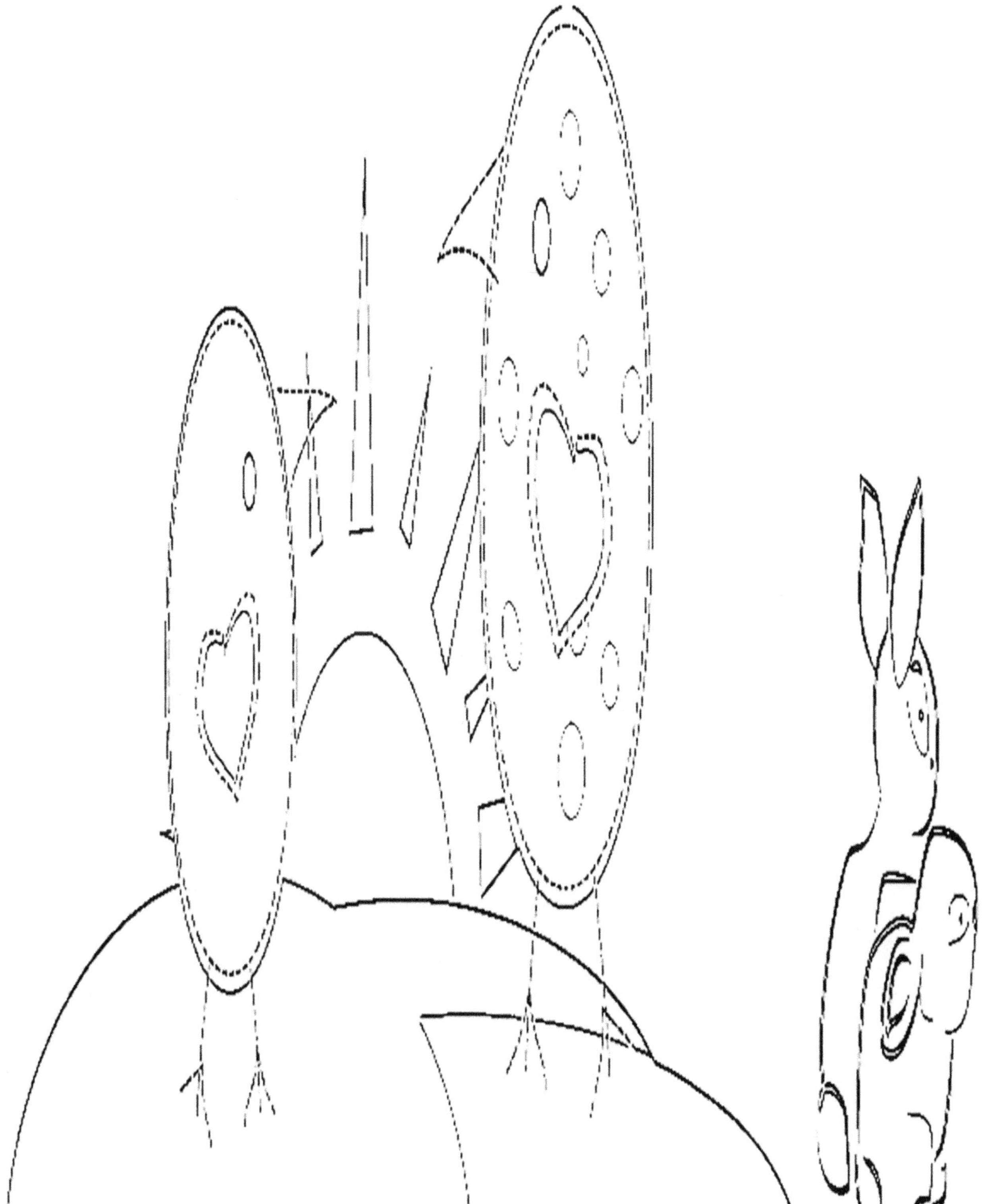

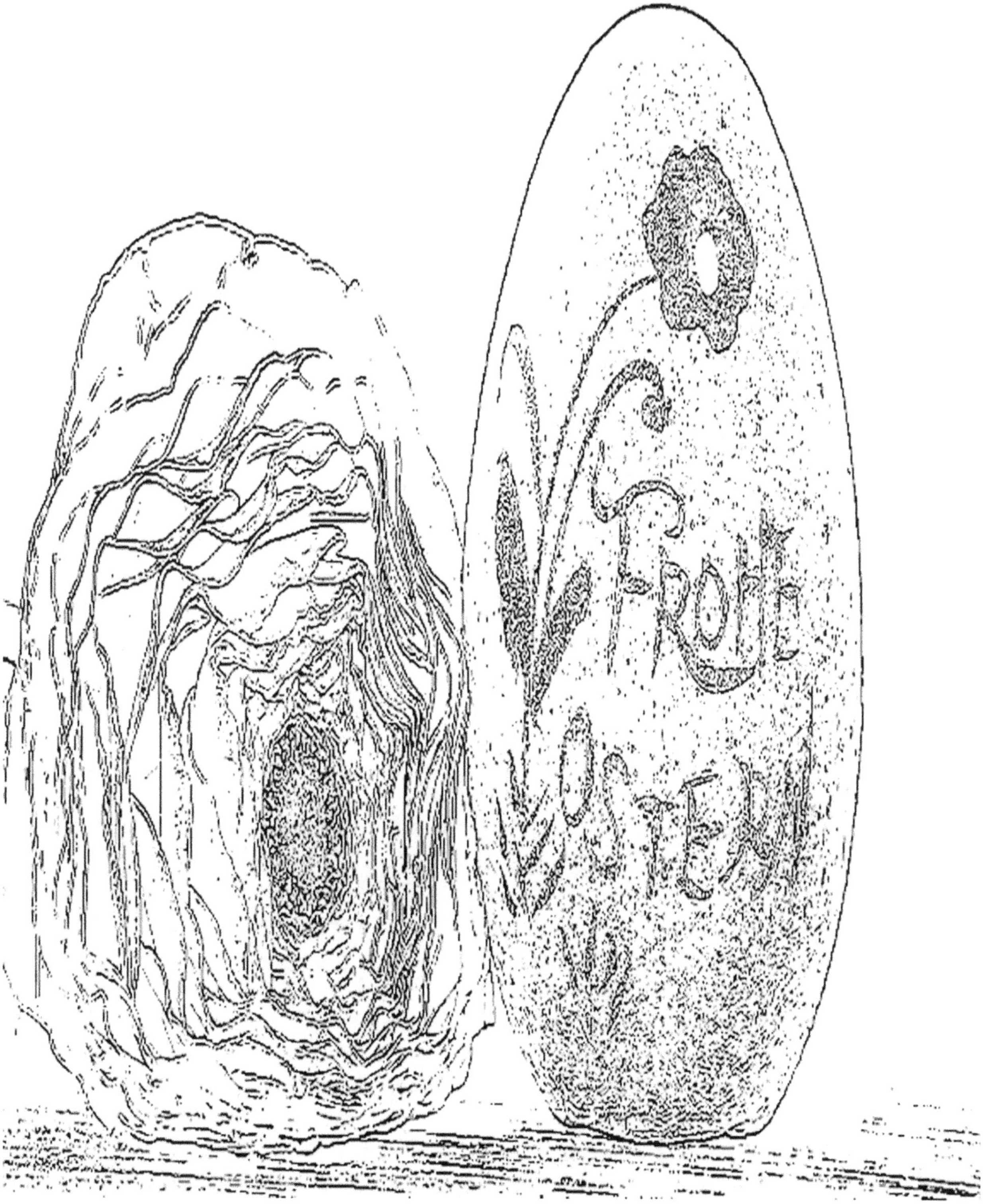
Frohe
Ostern

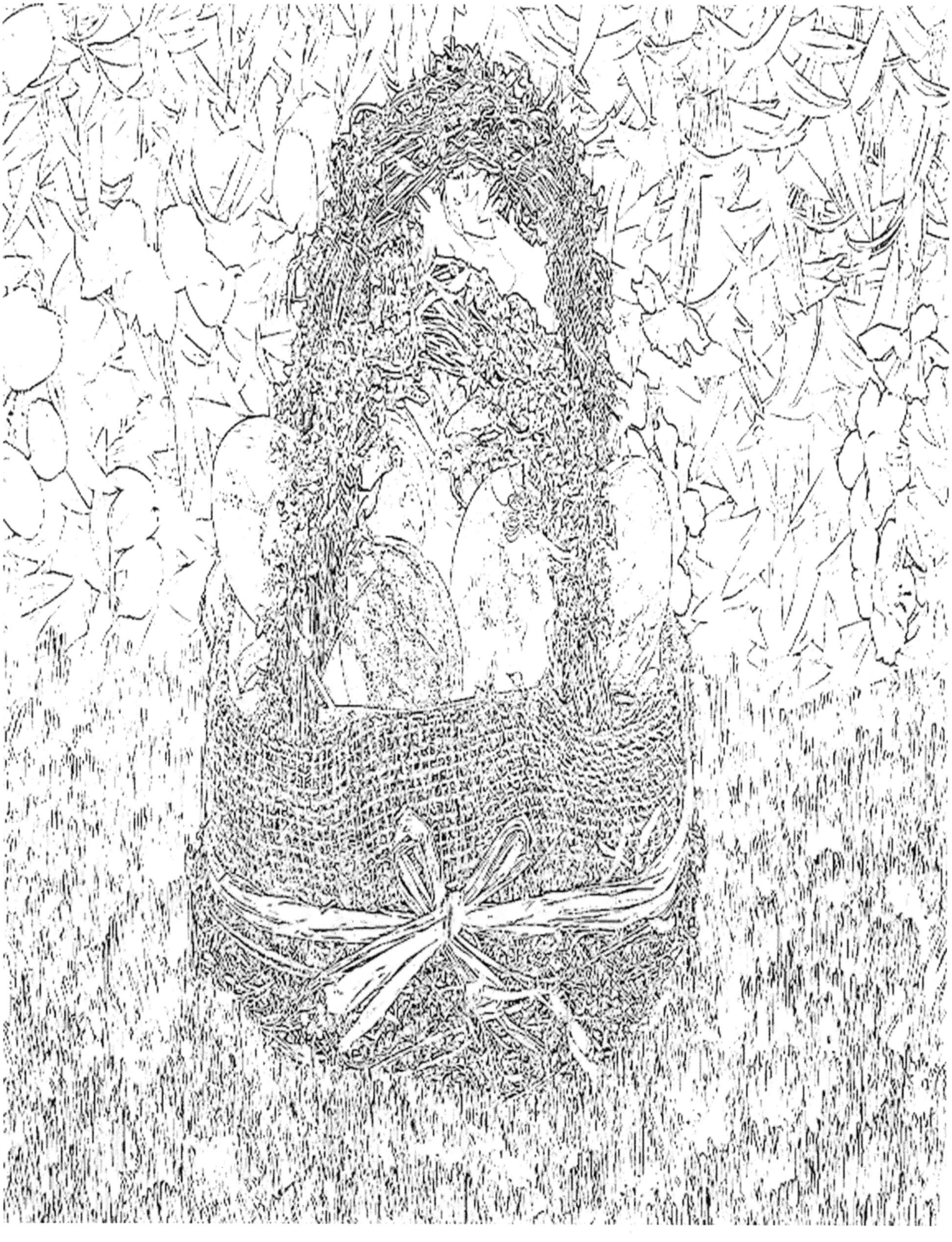

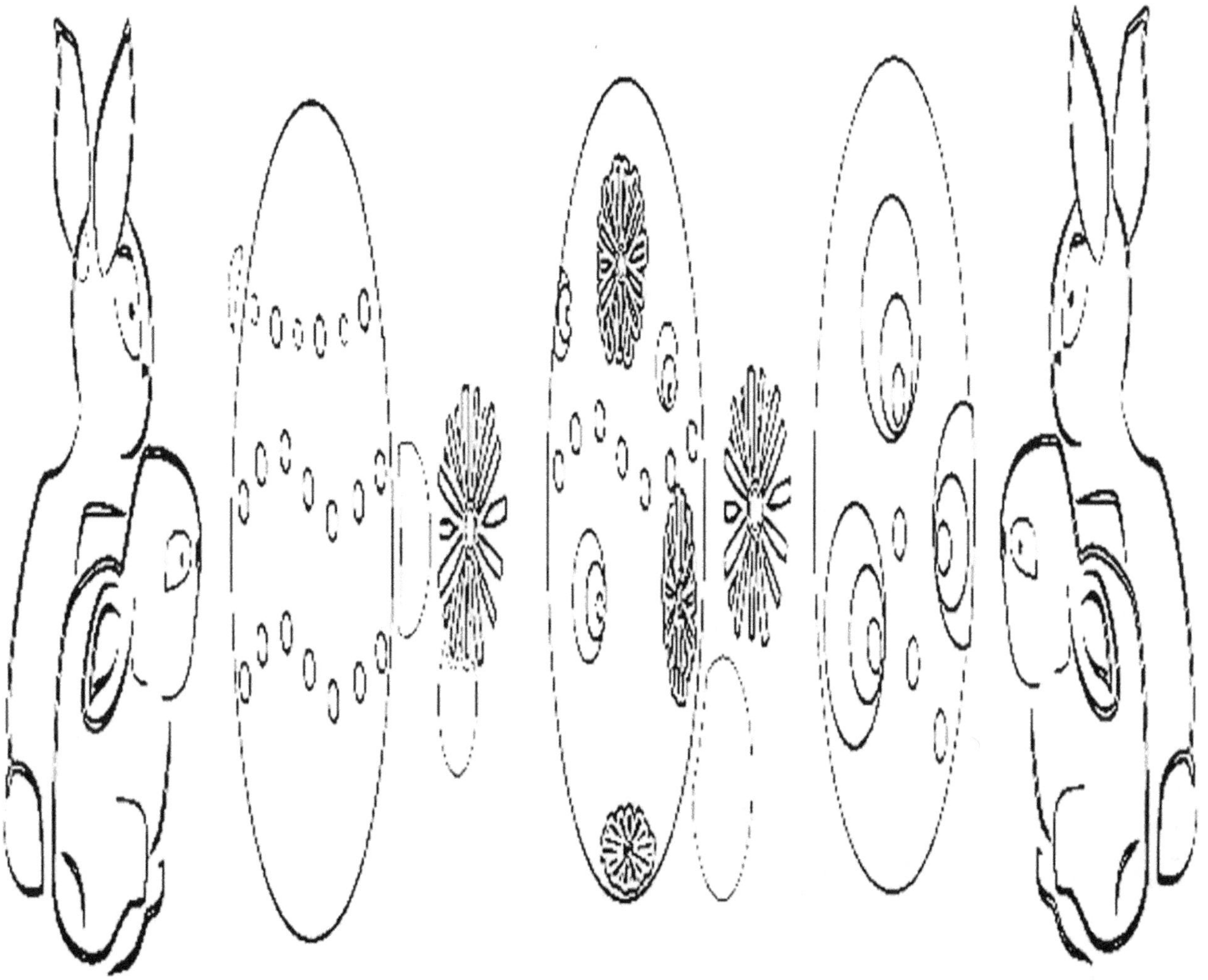

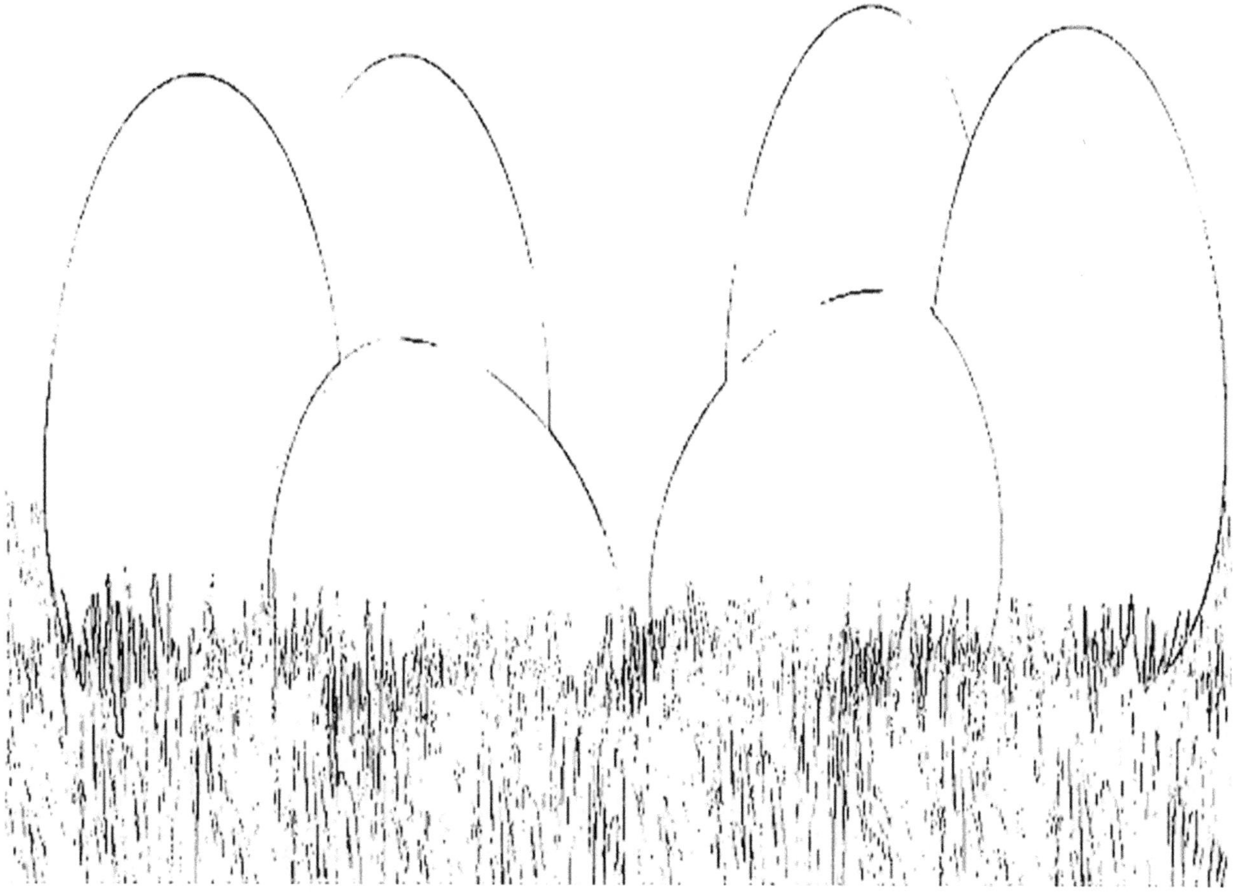

HAPPY EASTER

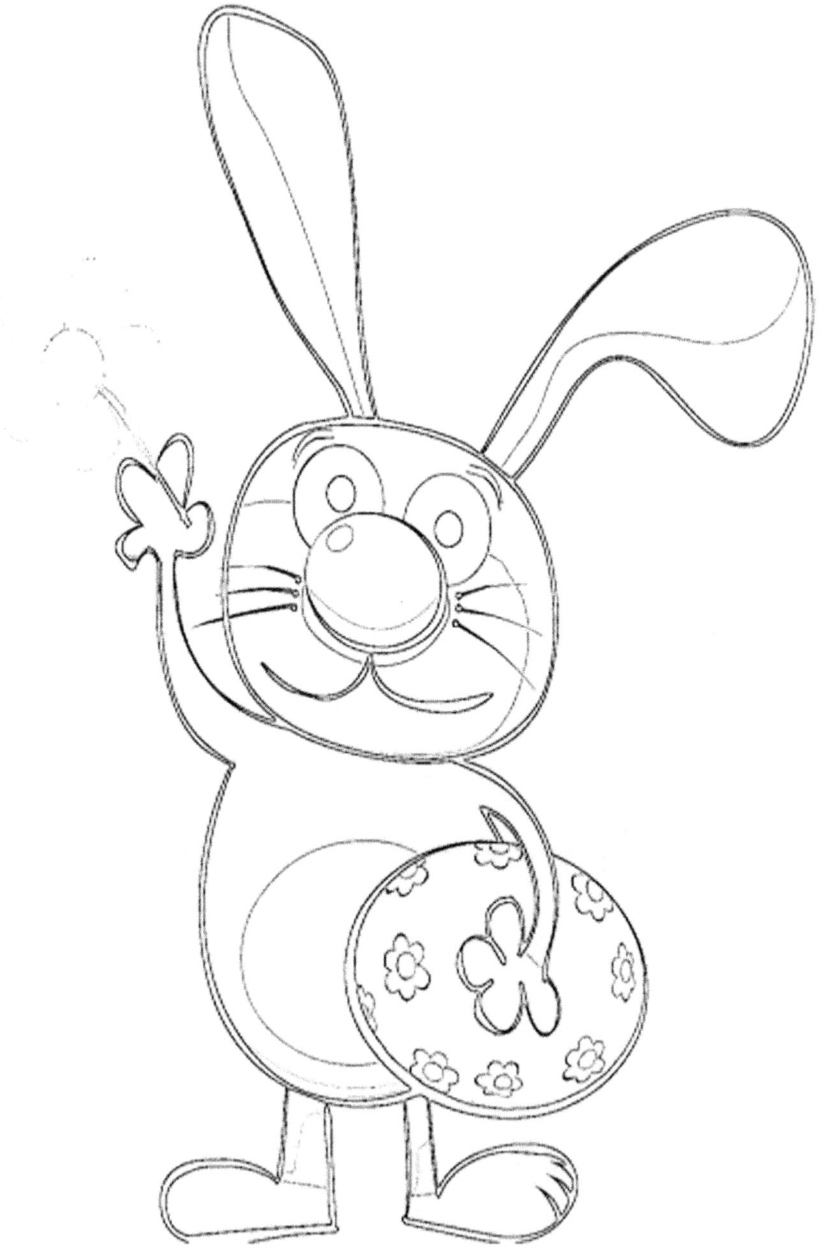

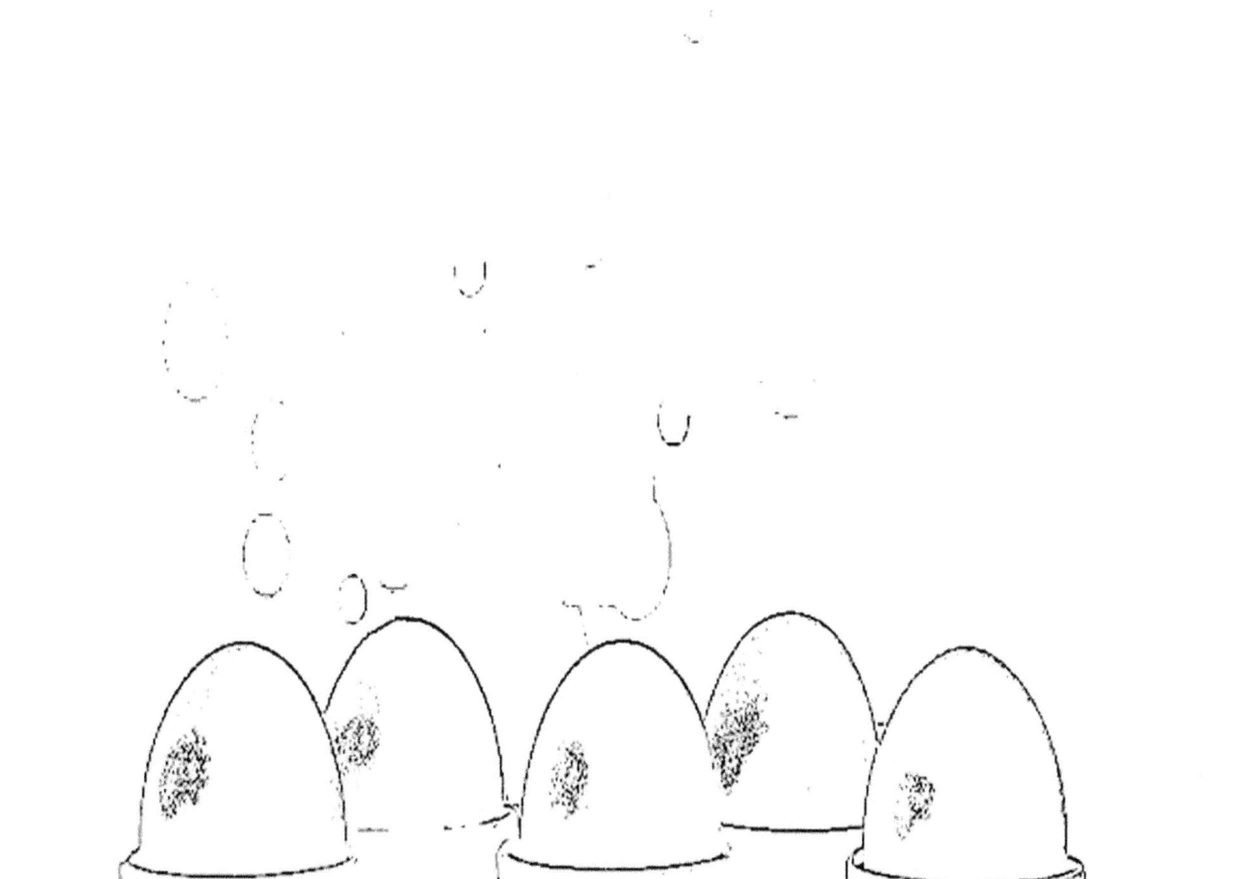

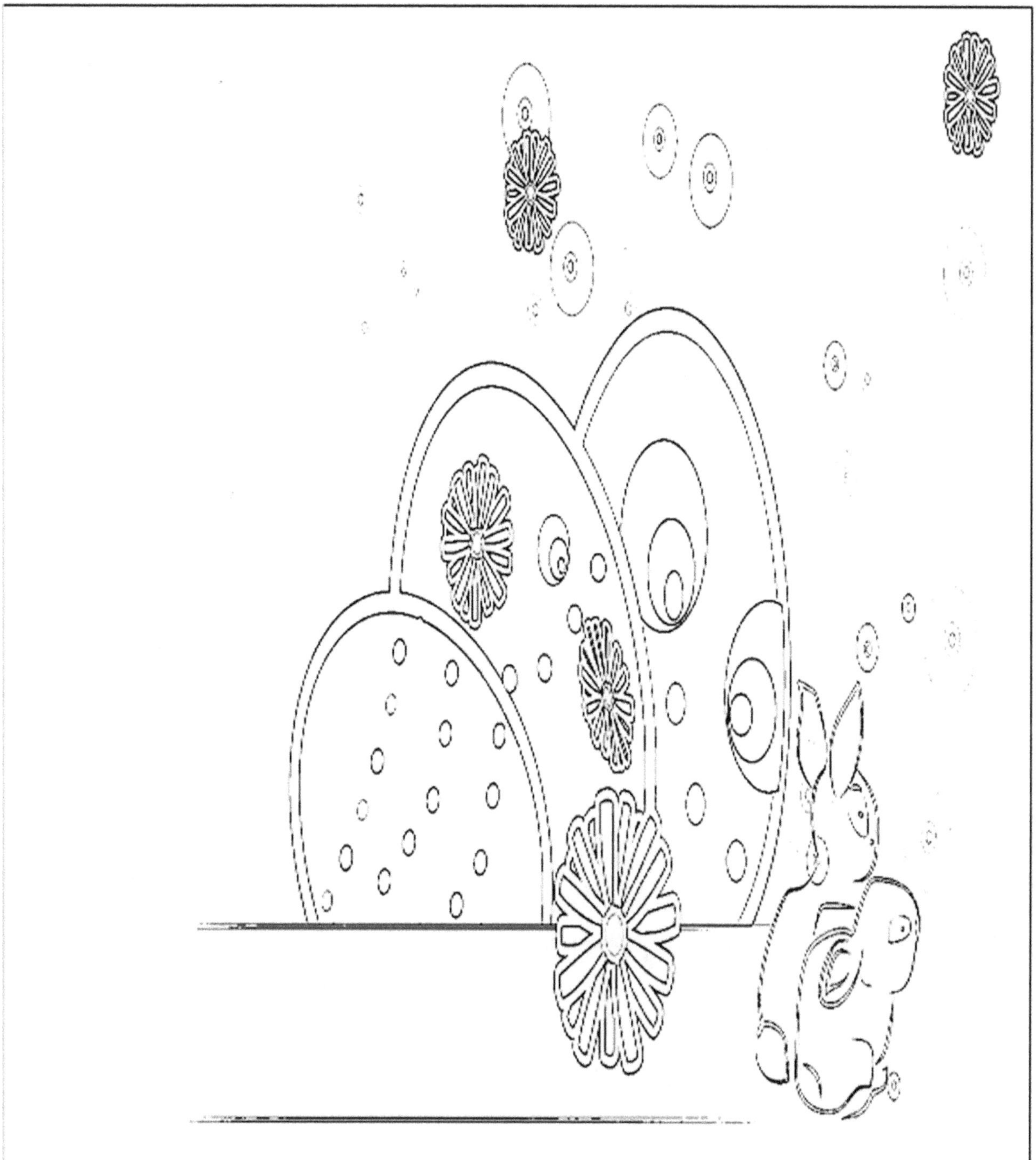

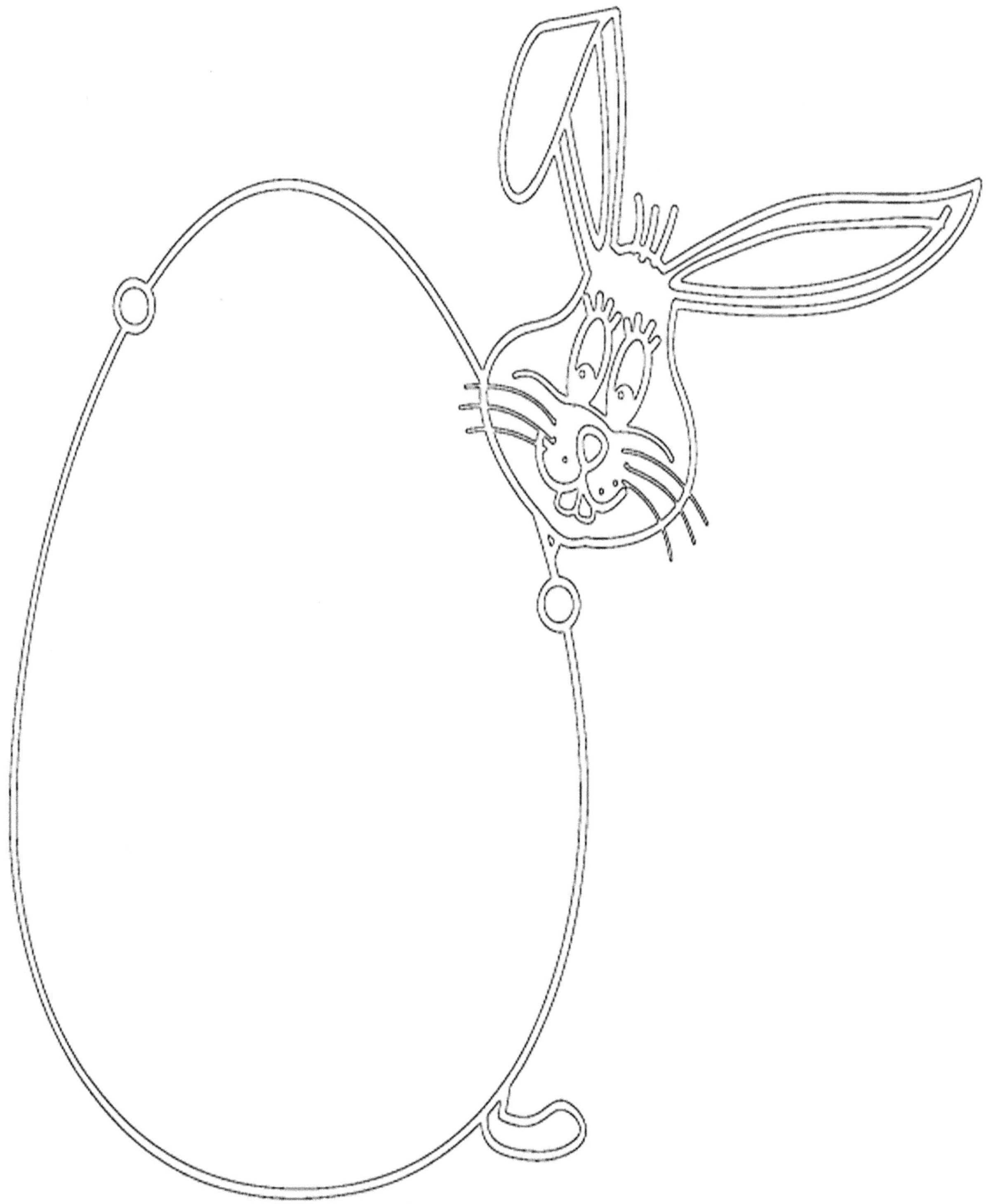

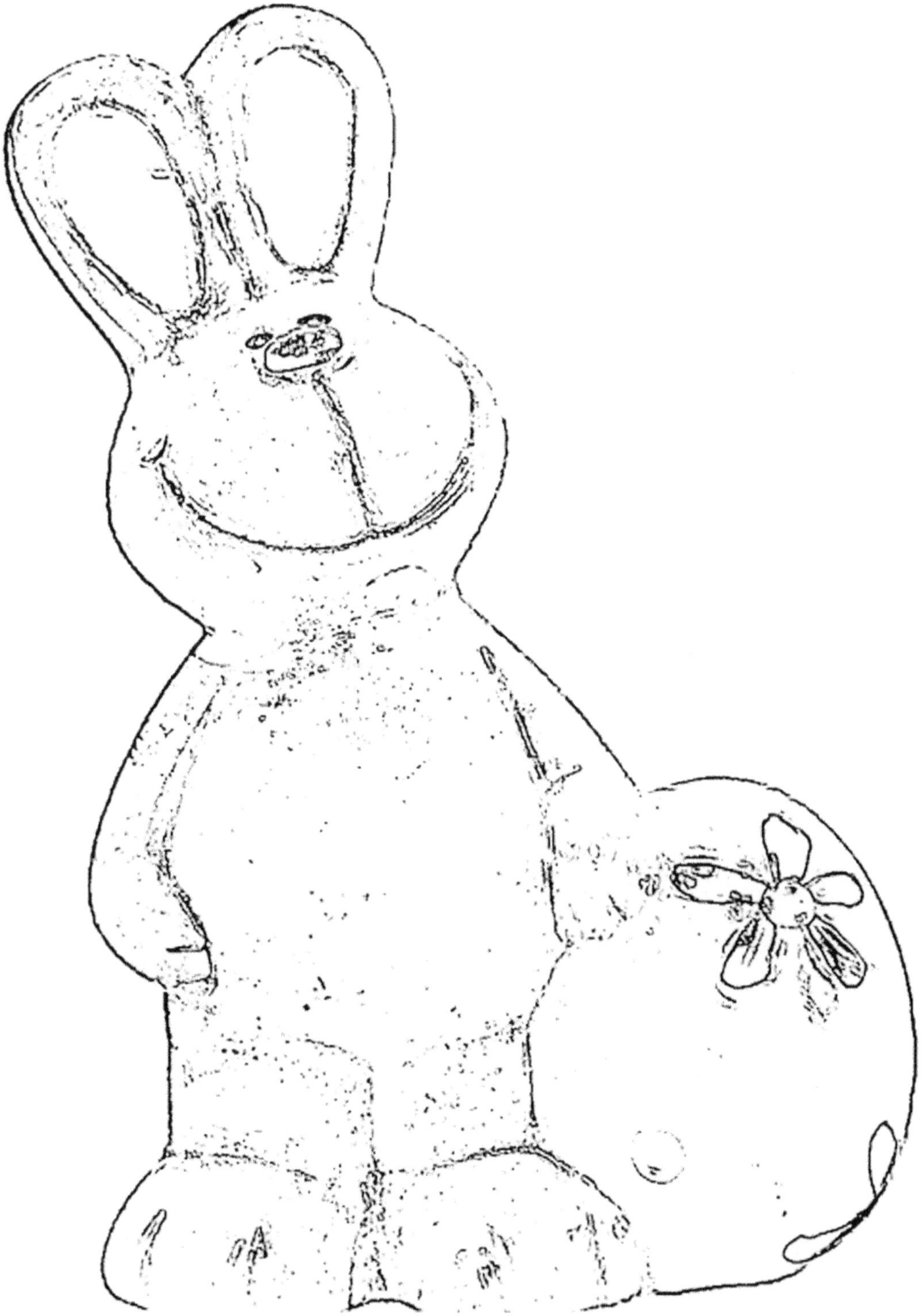

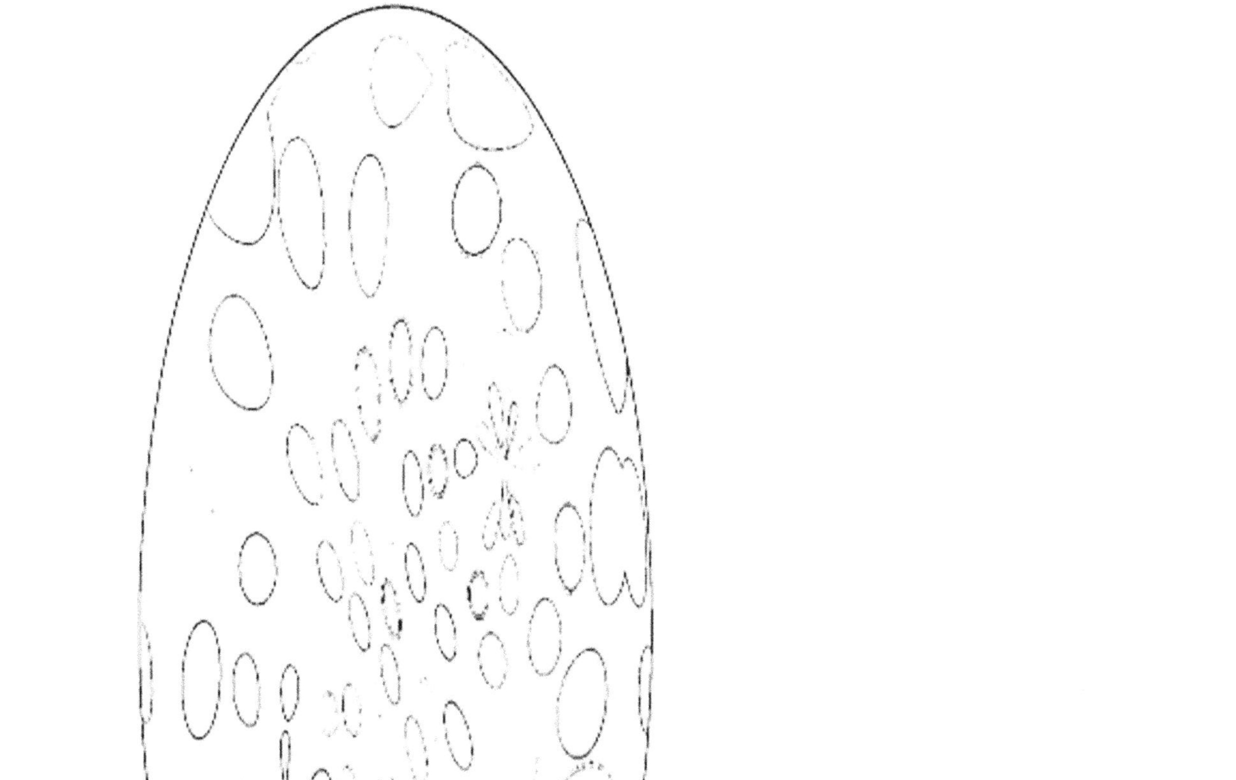

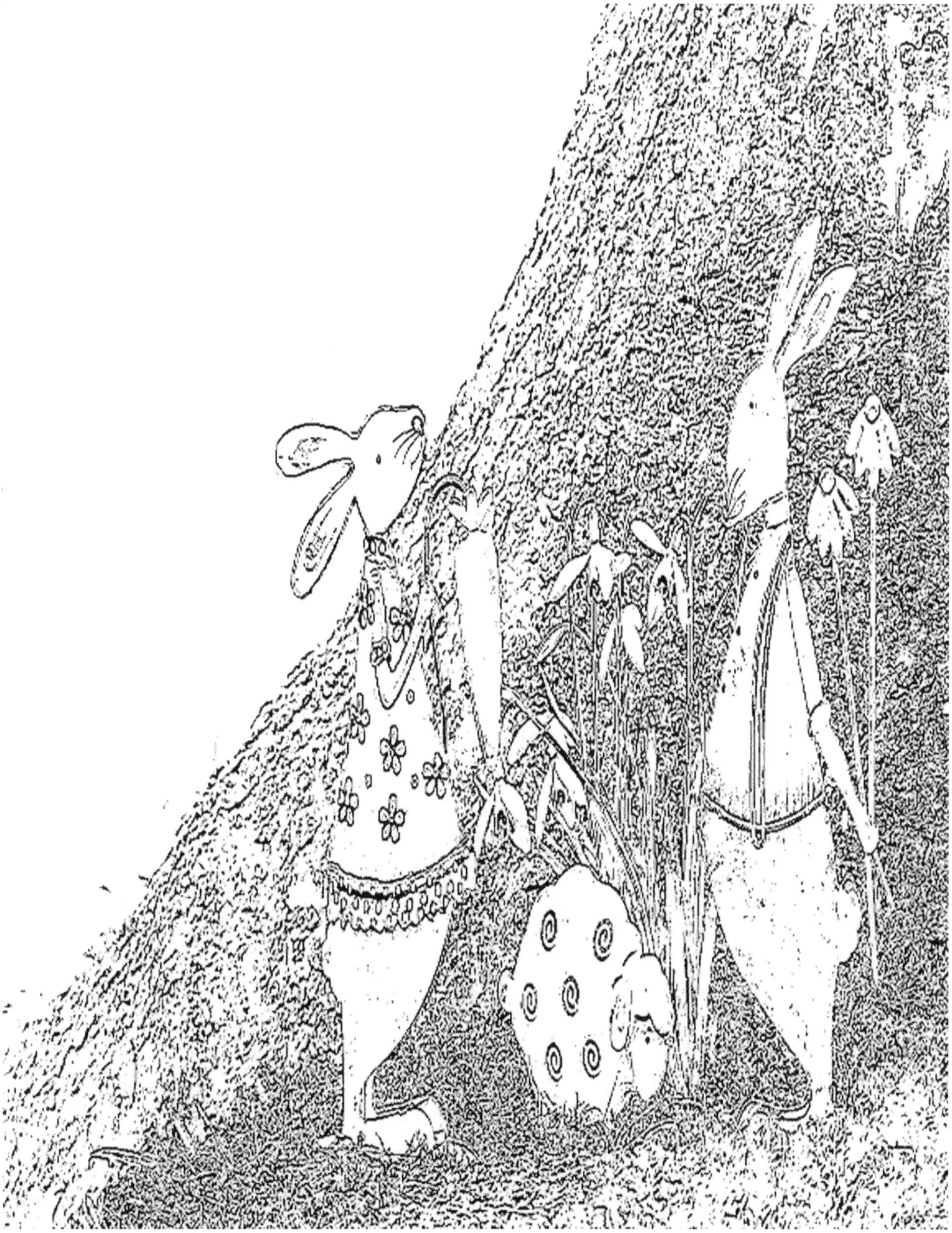

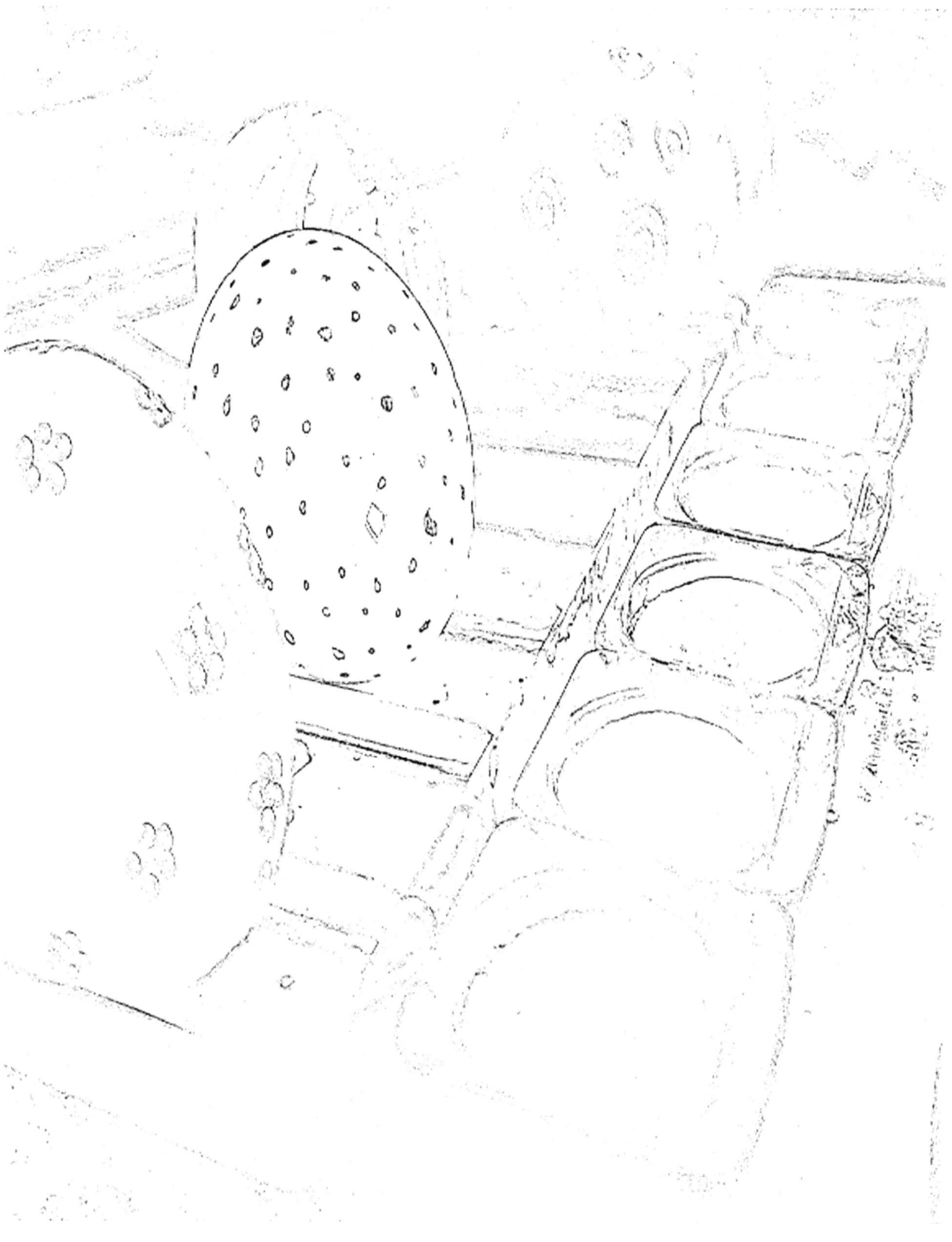

Note

www.ingramcontent.com/pod-product-compliance
Lightning Source LLC
Chambersburg PA
CBHW080631190526
45169CB00009B/3353
9781530507283